LIVING IN HIS SUFFICIENCY

BY

CHARLES F. STANLEY

THOMAS NELSON
Since 1798

NASHVILLE   DALLAS   MEXICO CITY   RIO DE JANEIRO

Published in Nashville, Tennessee, by Thomas Nelson, Inc.

Scripture quotations are from THE NEW KING JAMES VERSION. Copyright ©
1979, 1980, 1982, Thomas Nelson, Inc., Publishers.

ISBN 9781418541279

4 5 6 14 Q   G 13

Contents

David.

Our Sufficiency, Source, and Supply

Sufficiency—all that is needed in ample supply.

Supply—what is needed to meet a particular need, solve a particular problem, or overcome a particular lack.

Source—a fountainhead of supply that produces sufficiency.

These three terms—*sufficiency, supply*, and *source*—will be used almost interchangeably in this book because Jesus Christ is our Sufficiency for an abundant life, our Supply or Provision, and our Source of wholeness in this life and eternal life in the future. How do we know this? Because that is what the Bible teaches about Jesus Christ.

Countless other books tell about methods and means other than Christ as a foundation for wholeness, sufficiency, and everlasting supply. The Bible, however, is God's truth about who Jesus Christ is—really—and about what Christ provides for us. It is when we understand and apply what the Bible says that we truly come to know Christ Jesus as our Sufficiency. Make the Bible your ultimate authority on Jesus Christ and how to get your needs met, and you won't be disappointed!

This book can be used by you alone or by several people in a small group study. At various times, you will be asked to relate to the material in one of these four ways:

1. *What new insights have you gained?* Make notes about the insights that you have. You may want to record them in your Bible or in a separate journal. As you reflect back over your insights, you are likely to see how God has moved in your life.

1

2. *Have you ever had a similar experience?* Each of us approaches the Bible from a unique background—our own particular set of relationships and experiences. Our experiences do not make the Bible true—the Word of God is truth regardless of our opinion about it. It is important, however, to share our experiences in order to see how God's truth can be applied to human lives.

3. *How do you feel about the material presented?* Emotional responses do not give validity to Scripture, nor should we trust our emotions as a gauge for our faith. In small-group Bible study, however, it is good for participants to express their emotions. The Holy Spirit often communicates with us through this unspoken language.

4. *In what way do you feel challenged to respond or act?* God's Word may cause you to feel inspired or challenged to change something in your life. Take the challenge seriously and find ways of acting upon it. If the Lord reveals to you a particular need He wants you to address, take that as His "marching orders." He is expecting you to do something with the challenge He has just given you.

Start and conclude your Bible study sessions with prayer. Ask God to give you spiritual eyes to see and spiritual ears to hear. As you conclude your study, ask the Lord to seal what you have learned so that you will never forget it. Ask Him to help you grow into the fullness of the stature of Christ.

Again, I caution you to keep the Bible at the center of your study. A genuine Bible study stays focused on God's Word and promotes a growing faith and closer walk with the Holy Spirit in each person who participates.

LESSON 1

Where Do We Go for What's Missing?

❧ In This Lesson ❧

LEARNING: WHAT DO I FIND MISSING IN MY LIFE?

GROWING: HOW CAN I BE SURE THAT GOD WILL MEET ME IN MY NEEDS?

When you experience a crisis in your life, where do you turn *first*? When you recognize that something's missing in your life—when you have a lack of provision, security, hope, love, safety, comfort, or self-identity—from whom or what do you seek supply?

The answer to these questions for a Christian must be a resounding, "Lord Jesus!" To turn to any person, group, organization, or entity *other than* Christ for one's total provision and supply in life—both external and internal—is to deny, to some degree, the sufficiency of God.

❧ What do you feel is missing in your life at the moment? How does this missing element compare to your relationship with Christ?

How might your day-to-day life look different if you truly believed that Jesus meets all of your needs?

In the first century, false teachers made claims to new believers that Jesus Christ might be sufficient for some of their needs—perhaps even many or most of their needs—but that other traditional customs and beliefs were necessary *in addition to Christ* for a person to experience a total supply of all things. They taught that while He might be sufficient for a person's spiritual salvation, Jesus could not fulfill all practical, emotional, material, or social needs.

The apostle Paul soundly rejected the claims of these false teachers in his letter to the Colossians, which is entirely devoted to Paul's claim that Christ is 100 percent *sufficient* to meet all human needs, now and forever.

4

For this reason we also, since the day we heard it, do not cease to pray for you, and to ask that you may be filled with the knowledge of His will in all wisdom and spiritual understanding; that you may walk worthy of the Lord, fully pleasing Him, being fruitful in every good work and increasing in the knowledge of God.

—Col. 1:9, 10

"But what," you may ask, "does this have to do with me today? Paul was writing to people who lived in the ancient past, not the modern world." The same arguments that were made to the believers in the early church are being made to Christians and non-Christians today! The sufficiency of Christ is attacked from many sides, at times directly and boldly, and at times indirectly and with great subtlety. In my work as a pastor, I have encountered countless church-going believers who have fallen prey to arguments that Jesus is not sufficient to meet all of their needs. The main reason seems to be this: They do *not fully* know the Lord. Very specifically:

∾ They do not know the fullness of His deity.
∾ They do not have an intimate and ongoing, daily relationship with Him, which means they do not truly know Him—they only know about Him.

∾ What does it mean to know the fullness of Christ's deity?

❦ Why is it important to understand the deity of Christ? How can this understanding change your world view this week?

❦ Are you one who knows Jesus, or just knows about Him?

David.

The fact is, if we don't fully know Christ Jesus, we cannot know His sufficiency. And if we do not believe He is sufficient, and have an ability to access His sufficiency, we are vulnerable to arguments that can lead us astray—away from Christ and away from the perfection to which Christ calls us. On the other hand, if we have a deep understanding of all that He has provided for us and all that He makes available to us, we have a solid foundation on which to grow and develop in *every area of our lives.*

ꙮ Today and Tomorrow ꙮ

TODAY: A SOLID FOUNDATION, ONE ESTABLISHED ON THE ETERNAL PRINCIPLES OF GOD'S WORD, MUST BECOME MY DESIRE IN ORDER TO LIVE A MEANINGFUL, SATISFYING, AND VICTORIOUS LIFE.

TOMORROW: I WILL REMEMBER THAT GOD BECAME A MAN AND ENDURED ALL THAT I ENDURE.

Notes and Prayer Requests:

LESSON 2

Who Is Jesus . . . Really?

━━━━━━ ✍ In This Lesson ✍ ━━━━━━

LEARNING: WAS JESUS JUST A GOOD MAN?

GROWING: WHAT IS IT THAT I TRULY KNOW ABOUT GOD APART FROM JESUS?

Jesus made a tremendous claim about Himself in John 14:6 when He said: "I am the way, the truth, and the life. No one comes to the Father except through Me."

Countless people in our world refute this claim made by Christ, saying, "There are many paths to God. There are many religions, but as long as they all point in the same direction, they are to a great extent equal." Others are indignant at His claim, saying in effect, "How dare He think He is the only way to the Father." Still others try to discredit the claim of Jesus, saying that He didn't really mean what is written or that He didn't really say what John wrote. Genuine Christian believers through the ages, however, have staked their lives on this claim that Jesus made about Himself.

Our belief about Jesus Christ determines several important aspects of our faith:

- ✍ The relationship we believe we have with God
- ✍ How we respond to Jesus Christ
- ✍ How we live our lives in relationship to other people
- ✍ The power of our faith

 How do you respond to what Jesus said about Himself? What emotions does His statement cause you to feel?

 Why did Jesus say that He is the only way to God? Why does the world reject this teaching? What is your response to it?

David

Not a New Argument

The apostle Paul wrote the Book of Colossians to counter the arguments that were being circulated by a number of false teachers who claimed that Jesus was a good man but that belief in Him was not required or sufficient for salvation. These were teachers who advocated that other doctrines and cults had their place as equals to Christianity. In response to these false teachers, Paul said, "Don't let anyone delude you. Don't be misled!"

> Beware lest anyone cheat you through philosophy and empty deceit, according to the tradition of men, according to the basic principles of the world, and not according to Christ.

> —Col. 2:8

What are "the tradition of men" and "the basic principles of the world" today?

❧ How could a person be cheated by them?

Paul further responded to these false teachers by presenting two main arguments:

1. The false teachers have a wrong understanding about the deity of Jesus Christ. They do not understand that He truly was God incarnate, or God "in the flesh."
2. The false teachers have a wrong understanding about the blood of Jesus Christ and what His death on the Cross really meant. They do not understand the atonement that was made by Christ for the sins of all mankind.

Certainly it is not fully possible for any of us, in our finite human state, to comprehend the *fullness* of our infinite God. None of us are fully capable of comprehending the glory of the Trinity or the majesty of Jesus Christ. To a certain extent, all that we know about God the Father, Jesus Christ, and the Holy Spirit are things that we know *in part.* As Paul wrote to the Corinthians, "Now I know in part, but then I shall know just as I also am known" (1 Cor. 13:12).

Even so, there are some truths that we can know with certainty about God because Jesus Christ made those things very plain to us and explained them not only in words, but by the actions of His life. Paul made a concise and powerful statement about Jesus in the opening verses of his letter to the Colossians, which summarizes his teaching about *who* Jesus really was and is. These are facts about God that Paul knew with certainty:

He is the image of the invisible God, the firstborn over all creation. For by Him all things were created that are in heaven and that are on earth, visible and invisible, whether thrones or dominions or principalities or powers. All things were created through Him and for Him. And He is before all things, and in Him all things consist. And He is the head of the body, the church, who is the beginning, the firstborn from the dead, that in all things He may have the preeminence.

For it pleased the Father that in Him all the fullness should dwell, and by Him to reconcile all things to Himself, by Him, whether things on earth or things in heaven, having made peace through the blood of His cross.

—Col. 1:15–20

❧ Can you, like Paul, say that you know these things with certainty?

❧ What does it mean that Jesus is "the image of the invisible God"? The "firstborn over all creation"?

The Image of the Invisible God

Paul makes as his first statement about Jesus Christ that He is "the image of the invisible God" (Col. 1:15). The Hebrew people had long held to the belief that God was Spirit—invisible to man and clothed in brilliant light. Just as a person cannot look directly into the sun at high noon, so a person is incapable of looking fully and directly at the glory of God.

The Jews also believed, however, that God manifested Himself in humanlike form from time to time for the purposes of communicating eternal truth to mankind or to give certain prophets very specific direction or assistance. There are a number of instances in the Old Testament of "the Lord" having physical characteristics—a form that many Bible scholars term "the pre-incarnate Christ." For example, Jacob wrestled with Him; and Shadrach, Meshach, and Abed-Nego, three Hebrew captives in Babylon, walked with Him in a burning furnace. God put on a flesh-like appearance, but God the Father is *not* flesh.

Who is Jesus? Jesus is the incarnate Son of God. If you truly grasp this truth of God's Word, you can never think of Jesus again as just a good man. Jesus was and is God in fleshly form. All others who have claimed to be a "god" have been blemished, flawed, or tainted by sin in some way . . . but not Jesus. He was perfect, without sin. He was the "only begotten Son" of God (John 3:16). In His flesh, Jesus was fully man. In His Spirit—His nature, His character, His inner being—He was fully God. He was God clothed in human flesh, walking on this earth and showing us by His life—His words and deeds—the nature and will of God the Father.

For it pleased the Father that in Him [Jesus Christ] all the full-ness should dwell, and by Him to reconcile all things to Him-self.

—Col. 1:19, 20

For in Him dwells all the fullness of the Godhead bodily.

—Col. 2:9

Why Did God Reveal Himself as Jesus?

Why did Jesus come to this earth? What was the purpose of God re-vealing Himself in this way? One of the foremost reasons was so that we might truly *know* Him. God desired for mankind to know Him in a more intimate way—to know His heartbeat, mind, plans and purposes, nature and character. Read what the writer to the Hebrews said:

God, who at various times and in various ways spoke in time past to the fathers by the prophets, has in these last days spoken to us by His Son, whom He has appointed heir of all things, through whom also He made the worlds; who being the brightness of His glory and the express image of His person, and upholding all things by the word of His power.

—Hebrews 1:1–3

Jesus came to show us what God is like. He came to explain God to us. He came as the "express image" of God to speak to us God's words and to show us how God thinks, feels, and loves. So many people today say they know God, but they don't want anything to do with Jesus. That simply is not possible! Jesus was and is God. God cannot be known directly apart from Jesus. If you look at this world to know God apart from Christ, you're left with natural laws alone—and friend, nature does not give us a full or accurate picture of God because we live in a fallen world that has been greatly impacted by man's sinful nature. How can a person know about the love of God, the mercy of God, the joy of knowing God apart from Jesus Christ? It isn't possible. Jesus came to show us the Father in a way that we could fully understand. As a child once said, "Jesus is God with a face and arms."

Christ came to take away the veil of mystery from God's plan and purpose for mankind. If Jesus was not the Son of God—if He was not God, not deity—then He is not sufficient. But because Jesus is, indeed, God the Son, He is completely sufficient—for what need could we possibly have that God cannot meet, what lack could we possibly experience that God cannot fill, what problem could we possibly have that God cannot solve? God, who is all-powerful, all-wise, all-loving, and who is ever-present and eternal—God who knows the beginning from the ending and who controls and governs all things—is entirely sufficient. And Jesus is God.

❧ Today and Tomorrow ❧

TODAY: JESUS CAME TO MAKE GOD APPROACHABLE AND UNDERSTANDABLE TO THE HUMAN HEART AND MIND.

TOMORROW: I WILL ASK THE LORD TO KEEP ME EVER THANKFUL FOR JESUS' WORK ON THE CROSS, WHICH RECONCILED ME TO HIM.

∞ **Notes and Prayer Requests:** ∞

LESSON 3

All We Need for Reconciliation with God

❧ In This Lesson ❧

LEARNING: WHY DO I NEED TO BE RECONCILED TO GOD?

GROWING: IS THERE ANYTHING I CAN DO TO AFFECT MY POSITION BEFORE HIM?

Jesus not only came to show us what God the Father is like, but to reconcile us to God the Father. He accomplished this through His death on the Cross, making it possible for all who believe in Christ Jesus to be saved from eternal death. To become reconciled to God we need only believe in Jesus Christ as our Savior and to accept what He did on the Cross as being on our behalf. Jesus Christ is totally sufficient for our salvation.

There are those in various religions and even Christian denominations who claim that for a person to be fully reconciled to God, he must complete various rituals or fulfill certain types of works or obligations. But God's Word proclaims strongly that no amount of works, effort, or goodness on our part can bring about our salvation. In fact, no one and no thing other than Jesus Christ is the Savior. And furthermore, Jesus Christ is fully sufficient to be the Savior—nothing "in addition" to believing in Christ Jesus is necessary for a person to be born again spiritually, to receive God's forgiveness, and to experience the presence of the Holy Spirit.

A Full and Complete Reconciliation

What does it mean to be reconciled to someone, and in particular, to God?

First, the word *reconciliation* implies that a relationship has been broken and is in need of mending. We each are born into a state of estrangement or distance from God. With certainty, God loves us, He created us for Himself, and He desires to be reconciled with us—and this is true every second of our lives. But we each are born with the sin nature that is the inheritance of all human beings after the fall of Adam and Eve. This sin nature separates us from God since God can have no association with it. We also are given a free will by God from our birth so that we can choose to retain our old sin nature or turn to God, receive His forgiveness, and receive a new nature—one that is not rooted in sin.

When Jesus died on the Cross as our eternal, definitive, substitutionary sacrifice for sin, He made it possible for those who *accept* what Jesus did to have their sin nature changed and thus, be made *acceptable* for close intimacy with God the Father. Our part in bringing about reconciliation is to say to Him, "Father, I believe in Jesus Christ as my Savior. I accept what He did on the Cross as being for my sins. Please forgive me, change my sin nature, and fill me with Your Holy Spirit so I can live my life in a way that is totally pleasing to You."

Have you accepted the reconciliation that Jesus Christ makes possible? If not, I encourage you to do so today.

Reconciliation Brings Change

Believing in Jesus Christ brings about newness in a person. The old sin nature is no more. A new nature that desires the goodness and righteousness of God takes its place. We are no longer the spiritual sons of Adam, but we are the spiritual sons of God the Father. The change is *not* something we are required to work up on our own. It is not something we must strive to do. Rather, it is the work of Jesus Christ in our lives. He is the One who changes us, from the inside out.

Paul wrote very specifically about reconciliation and newness of spiritual life to the Colossians:

> For it pleased the Father that in Him all the fullness should dwell, and by Him to reconcile all things to Himself, by Him, whether things on earth or things in heaven, having made peace through the blood of His cross. And you, who once were alienated and enemies in your mind by wicked works, yet now He has reconciled in the body of His flesh through death, to present you holy, and blameless, and above reproach in His sight.
>
> —1:19–22

What does a life alienated from God look like?

⮟ How does that life contrast with one "above reproach"?

I want to call your attention to four words and phrases in the passage from Colossians:

1. Peace. So many people believe that God is in some kind of cosmic tug-of-war with mankind. God wants one thing, men and women want another, and God is acting as a harsh judge to whip mankind into shape. When you read the Bible closely, however, you will discover a wonderful truth: Jesus came to war against the devil and against evil, but He came to bring peace to the hearts of all who would believe in Him—not just a truce, but a lasting rest in our relationship so that we are no longer at odds with God. When we accept Jesus as Savior and receive His

Holy Spirit into our lives, we are made one with Christ and therefore, we are one with the Father. We begin to want what God wants and to desire what God desires.

So many people are looking in all the wrong places to find peace of heart and mind. They think they will find peace of heart by possessing certain things, reaching certain levels of achievement, taking certain chemicals into their bodies, or by entering into certain relationships. Genuine peace is to be found in only one place—in relationship with Jesus Christ. He is completely sufficient for our peace.

2. Holy. The word *holy* means "separate." Those who are indwelled by Jesus Christ are separate from those who do not believe in Jesus as Savior and Lord of their lives. When you accept Jesus and are born again, God no longer sees you as part of the teeming mass of sinful humanity but as His own child. He looks upon you the same way He looks upon Christ who dwells in you: You are His beloved son or daughter.

3. Blameless. To be blameless means that there are no eternal consequences associated with your old sin nature. In God's eyes, your salvation completely frees you from the eternal consequences of sin. God no longer remembers your sin once you accept His forgiveness. What freedom this brings to the person who fully grasps this truth!

4. Above reproach. To be above reproach means that God has no reservations whatsoever about associating with you. He longs to be with you, to spend time with you, to communicate with you, and to shower upon you His unending love. He desires an intimate, daily, walking-and-talking relationship with you.

> Just as He chose us in Him before the foundation of the world,
> that we should be holy and without blame before Him in love.
>
> —Eph. 1:4

23

How do you feel about being called holy, blameless, and above reproach before God?

Do you believe that it's true? How does your life reflect this?

What glorious identity we have with God the Father once we have accepted Jesus Christ as our Savior and have been reconciled to God through His shed blood!

"But what," you may ask, "does this mean to me in my everyday life?" It means that you no longer need to strive to get good enough for God. So many people today are trying to earn enough points to gain God's favor or to secure a home in heaven. Many are striving to do good works with the hope they will win God's love. God's Word says that all you need to do to be fully reconciled to God is to believe in Jesus Christ!

It also means you no longer need to be concerned about your own reputation or success. Now I don't mean that a person needs to stop working, planning, witnessing for Christ, or participating in worthwhile ministry activities. Rather, I mean that a person no longer needs to feel he is totally responsible for the *effectiveness* of what he does. God calls us to be faithful, and as we are faithful, He brings about the results of our faithfulness in His time, according to His methods, and always for His eternal purposes. The Lord may call you to preach or teach . . . but He is the One who converts the hearts of men and women. He may call you to pray for those in need . . . but He is the One who heals and makes whole. He may call you to give generously to the work of His kingdom . . . but He is the One who multiplies the gifts that are given and rewards those who give in ways that are beyond any taint of manipulation or calculation.

How would your life be different if you no longer felt the need to be concerned with your own reputation or success?

How can you go about making that a reality in your life?

Today and Tomorrow

TODAY: YOUR REPUTATION AND STANDING BEFORE GOD ARE SECURED 100 PERCENT BY JESUS CHRIST. HE IS THE ONE WHO IS AT WORK WITHIN YOU TO DO HIS GOOD PLEASURE.

TOMORROW: I WILL ASK THE LORD TO ENLARGE MY VIEW OF JESUS CHRIST—TRULY TO SEE HIM AS THE ONE WHO KNOWS ALL ABOUT ME, GOVERNS ALL THINGS AROUND ME, AND DESIRES TO BRING ABOUT THE FULLNESS OF MY LIFE.

All We Need to Feel Confident and Be Effective

◈ In This Lesson ◈

LEARNING: WHY DO I SEEK CONFIDENCE IN THINGS OTHER THAN CHRIST?

GROWING: HOW CAN I KEEP MYSELF FROM BEING BLINDED TO THE DEITY AND POWER OF JESUS?

Many people say that they would like to feel confident in a given situation or more confident in general. What is to be the basis for our confidence as Christians? Too often we look at certain outward traits as signs of confidence. For example, we tend to feel more confident if we are dressed well, know that we look acceptable, are with the "right" people, or feel that we have sufficient courage, information, or skill to face a given task.

Real confidence, however, arises from who we are on the inside. Confidence can be broken down into several traits:

- ◈ Having the power to be effective or to make a difference
- ◈ Having the resources necessary to be effective
- ◈ Having the insight, wisdom, or information necessary to make choices and decisions that truly matter and that make a difference in the lives of others, as well as ourselves
- ◈ Having the inner fortitude to endure criticism or ridicule and emerge on the side of right

- Having the status necessary to get a job done
- Having a reputation of past achievement
- Feeling a special calling of God to undertake a specific task, knowing by faith that we will succeed

Who is it that gives us such confidence?

Christ Jesus! Ultimately, Jesus is the only One who can give us genuine confidence and make us effective in all He leads us to undertake. As Christians, who we are on the inside relates directly to whom we have dwelling in us—Christ! This is not to discount the contribution of unconditional love from parents, teachers, and others in the life of a child, or the unconditional love received from others as an adult. However, Jesus Christ is the only One who can fully satisfy our needs for love, acceptance, belonging, competency, and worthiness.

The Source of Our Confidence

In Revelation 5:12, 13, we find the angels and elders of heaven saying with a loud voice around the throne of God:

> Worthy is the Lamb who was slain to receive power and riches and wisdom, and strength and honor and glory and blessing! And every creature which is in heaven and on the earth and under the earth and such as are in the sea, and all that are in them, I heard saying: "Blessing and honor and glory and power be to Him who sits on the throne, and to the Lamb, forever and ever!"

> —Rev. 5:12, 13

Jesus alone is worthy. He is the One from whom all power, riches, wisdom, strength, honor, glory, and blessing come! In other words, He is the One who imparts to us the power or strength that we may be lacking but that is required of us to be effective and to make a difference for good. He is the One who imparts to us the resources, wisdom, enduring strength, status, reputation, and faith-calling that we need to be effective. All the traits we desire as a part of "self-confidence" are resident in Jesus Christ, and they are imparted from Him to us.

How has Jesus met the need for various aspects of confidence in your life?

🕮 In your life, have you experienced times when you relied on someone or something other than Jesus as the foundation for your confidence? What was the result?

We can base 100 percent of our confidence on Christ for three reasons:

1. Jesus Christ alone knows who we are . . . completely.
2. Jesus Christ alone knows what is missing in our lives.
3. Jesus Christ alone can *supply* to us what is missing to make us whole and to make us effective.

Bethany Carla √ Debbie Jesus Christ Knows Us Completely

Jesus Christ knows us completely because He was with the Father when we were made. He knows exactly who we are, and what we are capable of being and doing, because He was present at our creation.

Paul wrote to the Colossians that Jesus was "the firstborn over all creation" (1:15). He also wrote,

For by Him all things were created that are in heaven and that are on earth, visible and invisible, whether thrones or dominions or principalities or powers. All things were created through Him and for Him. And He is before all things, and in Him all things consist.

—1:16, 17

What does it mean for Jesus to be the "firstborn"? "First," in this case, refers to position, preeminence, and power, not first in time or chronology. He is the firstborn "over" all creation, not the firstborn "of" creation. We refer to the wife of the President of the United States as the First Lady. This does not mean that she was the first president's wife, or the first woman ever to fill this position. It means she is considered to be in an elevated position of prestige. Jesus is the first, the preeminent, the most important, the most prestigious, the most revered, the most worthy.

Our Author and Finisher

Paul says that all things were created by Jesus Christ "through Him and for Him" (v. 16).

Jesus Christ is your "author." He knows the full story of your life, with all the details. He is your "finisher"—He is the One who can impart to you the power and ability to bring your story to its full completion (Heb. 12:2).

What does it mean to you and me to know that Jesus was present at our creation and that He knows *every* detail of our lives from start to finish? It means that nothing about us is a secret or a surprise to Jesus. He knows our present capacity, our future potential, all that is currently missing from our lives, and all that needs to be supplied and will be supplied so that we might accomplish God's purposes for us on earth!

Consider for a few moments the vastness and variety of God's creation. The orbits of all planets, stars, and galaxies are known by God and governed by Him. He made both gnat and elephant, tadpole and whale. He made the great variety of flowers and birds, and made each unique so that even the aroma of a yellow rose is not the same as that of a red one. He made each of His creatures with unique qualities and abilities. Consider for a few moments the intricacies of God's creation—all the systems and creatures exist in balance with one another. He made the spider to spin delicate webs and the breezes to carry pollen from one plant to the next.

God controls it all—tides and orbits and the clash of atoms in the invisible realm.

And this is the God who created *you*. He knows you inside and out. And what He made, He can remake. What He created, He can refashion. What He caused to come into being, He can heal, restore, and mend.

> Looking unto Jesus, the author and finisher of our faith, who for the joy that was set before Him endured the cross, despising the shame, and has sat down at the right hand of the throne of God.
>
> —Heb. 12:2

What does it mean that Jesus is the "author and finisher" of your faith?

🐦 What was "the joy that was set before Him"? What shame did Jesus face? Why did He do these things for your sake?

Created to Serve

Paul also wrote that we were created *for* Him. What does it mean for us to know that we were created by Christ and *for* Christ? You were not created to serve the devil or to serve yourself alone. You were created to serve Jesus Christ; you were created to praise Him, worship Him, and bring glory to His name. It also means that Christ Jesus has a plan for our lives. We do not need to wander aimlessly through life, without purpose or goals. God has a plan for us to fulfill. He has designed us to do a specific work on this earth for His purposes and His glory.

> For we are His workmanship, created in Christ Jesus for good works, which God prepared beforehand that we should walk in them.
>
> —Eph. 2:10

๛ What good works has God created for you to walk in?

Finally, a key aspect of Jesus Christ being our "Creator" means that Jesus was not only present at the time of our physical, natural creation—our conception and birth—but He was present at the time we received Him as our Savior. He was present at our spiritual re-creation, the time when we were born again. He is the One who makes all things new in our lives, the One who regards us as a "new creation" with a spiritual nature that is completely different from our old sin nature. It is Jesus Christ who transforms us spiritually, and it is for Him that we are to live spiritually.

> He was in the beginning with God. All things were made through Him, and without Him nothing was made that was made. In Him was life.

> —John 1:2–4

If anyone is in Christ, he is a new creation; old things have passed away; behold, all things have become new.

—2 Cor. 5:17

🌤 What old things have passed away?

🌤 What does it mean to you to be a new creation?

Jesus Christ Governs All Systems and Laws

Jesus Christ is not only the One who made you, but He is the One who governs all of the natural and spiritual systems and laws that impact your life. He created all things "visible and invisible, whether thrones or dominions or principalities or powers" (Col. 1:16). This means that all natural laws were created by Him and continue to be governed by Him. He holds all things together by the power of His Word! And not only laws that relate to the earth as we know it, but to processes in the emotional and spiritual realm that govern our relationships and the effectiveness of our prayers and our faith. Jesus Christ is the Lord of all.

Look again at Colossians 1:15–20, and this time circle or highlight each time the word *all* appears:

> He is the image of the invisible God, the firstborn over all creation. For by Him all things were created that are in heaven and that are on earth, visible and invisible, whether thrones or dominions or principalities or powers. All things were created through Him and for Him. And He is before all things, and in Him all things consist. And He is the head of the body, the church, who is the beginning, the firstborn from the dead, that in all things He may have the preeminence. For it pleased the Father that in Him all the fullness should dwell, and by Him to reconcile all things to Himself, by Him, whether things on earth or things in heaven, having made peace through the blood of His cross.

What does it mean to you and me to have *all* things governed by Jesus Christ? It means that all processes, procedures, systems, and laws are subject to Jesus Christ. He can use any method He desires to bring us the things we need. He can tap any resource and any system to bring us the power, ideas, information, courage, resources, help, energy, or creativity that may be necessary for us to fulfill God's plan for our lives.

🐾 How do you feel about Jesus Christ governing all things?

🐾 What new insights do you have into Christ's sufficiency?

Our Response to His Sufficiency

Many people do not put their entire trust and confidence in Jesus Christ for one main reason: Satan has blinded them to the deity and power of Christ. Paul wrote to the Corinthians:

> Even if our gospel is veiled, it is veiled to those who are perishing, whose minds the god of this age has blinded, who do not believe, lest the light of the gospel of the glory of Christ, who is the image of God, should shine on them.

Can you Be a Christian + still not trust?

> —2 Cor. 4:3, 4

When people are blinded to Christ's presence, nature, and identity, and they do not fully recognize who He is, they tend to make their own "gods." Such gods are always on their side, always do what they want, and always approve of their desires. However, once we recognize fully the nature, character, and identity of God the Son, Jesus Christ, we are freed from striving to "work up" confidence and effectiveness.

Paul prayed for the Ephesians that this would be their response to the sufficiency of Christ:

> That the God of our Lord Jesus Christ, the Father of glory, may give to you the spirit of wisdom and revelation in the knowledge of Him, the eyes of your understanding being enlightened; that you may know what is the hope of His calling, what are the riches of the glory of His inheritance in the saints, and what is the exceeding greatness of His power toward us who believe.

> —Ephesians 1:17–19

Note the three things Paul longs for them to have:

1. A complete understanding so they will know the *hope* of God's calling on their lives—in other words, they will know the future and the destiny that God built into their very creation.
2. The riches of their inheritance as believers in Christ Jesus—fully to know and receive all that Christ makes available to them to help them fulfill their God-given plan and purpose.
3. The greatness of Christ's power through the Holy Spirit to help them become, say, and do all that He desires for them to become, say, and do.

☙ Today and Tomorrow ❧

TODAY: JESUS CHRIST IS TRULY ADEQUATE FOR ALL THINGS.

TOMORROW: I WILL ASK THE HOLY SPIRIT TO BE MY SUFFICIENCY, DAY BY DAY.

∾ **Notes and Prayer Requests:** ∾

LESSON 5

All We Need to Live a Godly Life

───────── ❧ In This Lesson ☙ ─────────

LEARNING: WHAT ROLE DOES THE HOLY SPIRIT PLAY IN MY LIFE?

GROWING: HOW CAN I TRUST HIM TO BE MY SUFFICIENCY?

What happens when we receive Jesus Christ as Savior and are born again spiritually? Several things happen simultaneously:

❧ We receive God's complete forgiveness—the old sin nature is replaced with a new nature that desires His righteousness. All consequences for past sins are erased.

❧ We receive the gift of eternal life with God, a heavenly home forever.

❧ We usually experience a deep and abiding sense of peace and joy, although this may come over time as we realize more and more what God has done for us.

❧ We receive the Holy Spirit into our lives.

It is this last aspect of our spiritual birth that is the focus for this lesson. The Holy Spirit—sent by Jesus to dwell within all those who believe in Him—is the One who enables us to live a godly life every day for the rest of our lives. The Holy Spirit, which is the very Spirit of Christ Himself imparted to us in an unlimited form, is with us always. He is our sufficiency as we seek to walk in the footsteps of Jesus.

A Spiritual Transformation

Being born again involves a spiritual transformation. This transformation is as complete in the spiritual realm as the physical birth of a person. Just as a baby goes from being a fetus to an infant, so a person is changed spiritually from the old spiritual nature to the new nature when he accepts Jesus Christ as his Savior. What is it about our spirit that is changed? While God the Father is not made in *our* physical form, we nevertheless are made in *His* likeness. Genesis 1:26, 27 says:

> Then God said, "Let Us make man in Our own image, according to Our likeness" . . . So God created man in His own image; in the image of God He created him; male and female He created them.

The part of us that is God-like is certainly not our body. The part of us that is made in God's image is our inner part—and very specifically, our ability to think, our ability to feel, and our free will with which we make decisions and choices. While we will never have the infinite power, wisdom, or love of God, we have been created in His image to manifest power, wisdom, and love. When we are born again, we *think* differently, we *feel* differently, and our will *is* changed so that we begin to think as God thinks, feel as God feels, and make decisions and choices as God would make them. We begin to love others as God loves them.

 What difference has the Holy Spirit made in your life as a believer in Christ Jesus?

42

🐟 What does it mean that you are created in God's image? How does this fact influence your life?

The born-again person has an ability to respond *as God does* to any particular situation or circumstance. We, therefore, are made capable of saying what God would say and doing what God would do. We become a vessel in which and through which God might manifest His awesome power, wisdom and love. Because when we confess our sins to God and receive His forgiveness, we simultaneously receive His very presence into our lives in the form of the Holy Spirit. Jesus spoke about this when He said to His disciples, "You shall be baptized with the Holy Spirit . . . you shall receive power when the Holy Spirit has come upon you; and you shall be witnesses to Me in Jerusalem, and in all Judea and Samaria, and to the end of the earth" (Acts 1:5, 8).

Jesus also had this to say about the Holy Spirit—Jesus' very own Spirit—coming to be *in* us:

> I do not pray for these alone, but also for those who will believe in Me through their word; that they all may be one, as You, Father, are in Me, and I in You; that they also may be one in Us, that the world may believe that You sent me. And the glory

> which You gave Me I have given them, that they may be one
> just as We are one: *I in them,* and You in Me; that they may be
> made perfect in one.
>
> —John 17:20–23 (emphasis added)

One of the main themes of the apostle Paul's ministry was "Christ in me." He wrote and taught repeatedly about the Spirit residing within us, enabling us to live a godly life. As you read the three passages below, reflect on the difference the Holy Spirit makes in a believer's life:

> You are not in the flesh but in the Spirit, if indeed the Spirit of
> God dwells in you. Now if anyone does not have the Spirit of
> Christ, he is not His. And if Christ is in you, the body is dead
> because of sin, but the Spirit is life because of righteousness.
> But if the Spirit of Him who raised Jesus from the dead dwells
> in you, He who raised Christ from the dead will also give life to
> your mortal bodies through His Spirit who dwells in you.
>
> —Rom. 8:9–11

> For as many as are led by the Spirit of God, these are sons of
> God. For you did not receive the spirit of bondage again to fear,
> but you received the Spirit of adoption by whom we cry out,
> "Abba, Father."
>
> —Rom. 8:14, 15

> Do you not know that you are the temple of God and that the
> Spirit of God dwells in you?
>
> —1 Cor. 3:16

What does it mean to be the temple of God?

Does that affect your life of worship? If so, how?

One of the most wonderful truths in the Bible is this: As a believer in Jesus Christ, you have been indwelled by the very Spirit of Christ Jesus. God the Holy Spirit dwells inside your mortal flesh!

The Seal of the Holy Spirit

The Holy Spirit functions to "seal" us into the life of Christ Jesus. In Bible times, a seal served two functions. First, a seal was used to secure a document or object. The Holy Spirit's presence in our life "seals" us, securing us from any attempts of the devil to claim our souls for eternity. We are marked as God's own forever once we are indwelled by the Holy Spirit. Nothing and nobody can cause the Holy Spirit to depart from our lives. His sealing of us is absolute and lasting.

Second, a seal in Bible times was used to declare the ownership of an object. Seals were individually made, and no two seals were alike. In the Gospel of Mark, Jesus was asked whether the Jews should pay taxes to Rome. Jesus asked for a coin. He then said to them, using the coin as an example, "Render to Caesar the things that are Caesar's, and to God the things that are God's" (Mark 12:17). Jesus was saying that the person whose seal or "image" is on an item is the owner of the item. When the Holy Spirit places His seal on our lives, we are identified as belonging to Christ.

Now He who establishes us with you in Christ and has anointed us is God, who also has sealed us and given us the Spirit in our hearts as a guarantee.

—2 Cor. 1:21, 22

 What does it mean that God has given us the Spirit "as a guarantee"?

 How do you feel about being "sealed" in Christ Jesus by the Holy Spirit?

The Holy Spirit Convicts of Sin

Those who genuinely have been born again do not have a desire to sin. Their desire is to do the will of God the Father. Those who willfully choose to sin or to continue to sin deny the Lordship of Jesus Christ; they commit idolatry—choosing to follow and put their trust in something or someone other than Christ. The apostle John wrote that those who have been born anew have a different "seed" in them from those who still have a sinful nature—they bear the "seed" of Jesus Christ and because of this, they desire purity, righteousness, and obedience. John wrote:

> For this purpose the Son of God was manifested, that He might destroy the works of the devil. Whoever has been born of God does not sin, for His seed remains in him; and he cannot sin, because he has been born of God.
>
> —1 John 3:8, 9

This does not mean that a Christian *cannot* sin, but rather, that a Christian does not willfully choose to sin. As soon as a believer in Christ Jesus recognizes his sin, he seeks immediately to confess that sin, receive forgiveness for it, and to repent, which means to change one's will and to seek to obey God fully.

The Holy Spirit is quick to convict the believer of sin—not so that the believer's life might be miserable under the load of condemnation, but rather, so that the believer might quickly confess sin, be forgiven for it, and move forward in his life *without* guilt, shame, or feelings of condemnation. Furthermore, the Holy Spirit enables a believer to withstand future sinful temptations and to withstand evil.

᪑ Have you experienced the work of the Holy Spirit in your life to convict you of sin and help you withstand the temptation to sin? Have you noticed a change in your desire to sin since you accepted Christ into your life?

The Holy Spirit Leads and Guides

In several passages of Scripture, Jesus refers to the Holy Spirit as the "Spirit of truth." The Holy Spirit leads us to decisions, choices, and an understanding of God's will that is "right" or true from God's perspective. He empowers us both to *know* and to *keep* God's commandments. In fact, John wrote that one of the ways we can know that the Holy Spirit dwells within a person is that the person keeps God's statutes (see 1 John 3:24).

The Holy Spirit leads us in such a way that over time, believing, saying, and doing the right thing become as natural to us as breathing. The more we rely upon the help of the Holy Spirit to guide us into all truth and to lead us into the path of God's perfect will, the more we take on the character of Christ and the more we automatically seek to do what is pleasing in God's sight. Stop to think for a moment—a mother bird doesn't *teach* its baby birds to build nests. Neither do mother squirrels teach baby squirrels that winter's coming so it's time to gather and store food. God's creatures have a built-in instinct to do what must be done. So, too, the Holy Spirit becomes our built-in instinct for doing what is right in God's eyes. He is our Teacher and our Counselor.

☙ Can you recall an experience in your life in which the Holy Spirit led you into a right decision or guided you into a right choice?

☙ In what ways has the Holy Spirit helped you to obey God's commandments?

The Holy Spirit Makes Us Effective

The Holy Sprit makes our witness of Christ effective. As we noted at the beginning of this lesson, Jesus told His disciples that when they were baptized with the Holy Spirit, they would "receive power . . . and you shall be witnesses to Me" (Acts 1:8). The Holy Spirit is the One who makes our prayers effective, who causes our sharing of the gospel to prick the conscience of the nonbeliever, and who causes our ministry efforts to meet needs in the lives of others. No person can save a soul, no person can heal a body, no person can make another person whole—but Jesus can and does these works *if we will be faithful in sharing God's love and the message of salvation* with those who need to receive it.

> Most assuredly I say to you, he who believes in Me, the works that I do he will do also; and greater works than these he will do, because I go to My Father. And whatever you ask in My name, that I will do, that the Father may be glorified in the Son. If you ask anything in My name, I will do it.
>
> —John 14:12–14

> Likewise the Spirit also helps in our weaknesses. For we do not know what we should pray for as we ought, but the Spirit Himself makes intercession for us with groanings which cannot be uttered. Now He who searches the hearts knows what the mind of the Spirit is, because He makes intercession for the saints according to the will of God.
>
> —Rom. 8:26, 27

🕭 Do you ever feel hindered by your own limitations in ministry?

🕭 What do the above verses say in response to that?

How is it that we are to respond to God the Holy Spirit dwelling within us? By inviting Him to *be* our sufficiency day by day. The reason so many Christians seem to stumble and falter in their Christian walk is because they simply are too proud to acknowledge that they *need* God the Holy Spirit at all times and in all decisions and choices. The truth is, we can't do *anything* by ourselves in our own human strength. We cannot make our heart beat one additional beat or add one fraction of an inch to our height.

✎ Today and Tomorrow ✎

TODAY: THE HOLY SPIRIT WITHIN ME *IS* LIFE. IT IS UP TO ME TO INVITE HIM TO DO HIS WORK IN ME AND THROUGH ME.

TOMORROW: I WILL REMEMBER THAT GOD MEETS ALL MY DAILY NEEDS.

❧ **Notes and Prayer Requests:** ❧

Lesson 6

All We Need for Total Provision

In This Lesson

Learning: What are the things I desire most in life?

Growing: Why does God not answer all of my prayers?

Have you ever stopped to consider that nobody else can do what Jesus can do? Nobody else can save a soul, deliver a person from evil, heal the body, mind, or emotions, create abiding and lasting peace and joy in the human heart, or make a person whole. Human efforts can help set the stage for Jesus Christ to do His work, but no human being can do what He can do!

Isn't it amazing, then, that we *think* we can meet our physical and material needs apart from Jesus? So many people are attempting to do just that! Many Christians seem to believe that Jesus Christ can meet all spiritual needs, but when it comes to the meeting of their physical, emotional, or material needs, they need to look to something other than or something in addition to Him.

The fact is, however, that none of us can create any form of lasting provision or security for ourselves in the physical or material realm. Stock markets rise and fall, jobs are secured and lost, clients come and go, vendors change, children grow up and leave home, loved ones die, government policies and laws are revised, methods change, crime occurs, disease strikes . . . nothing stays the same forever except Jesus Christ.

A second major truth about the sufficiency of Christ is this: There is no need too great or too small for Jesus to meet it *completely*. We can never face a problem He can't solve, a question He can't answer, or a need He can't fulfill.

🕮 When reflecting back on your life, in what have you put your trust for security or provision other than Christ Jesus? What were the results?

🕮 Can you cite any area of need that Jesus was incapable of meeting?

External and Internal Provision

The New Testament writers were very clear in their understanding that Jesus would meet *all* of their needs, both external and internal. The apostle Paul wrote to the Philippians, "My God shall supply all your need according to His riches in glory by Christ Jesus" (Phil. 4:19). Paul did not place any qualifications upon the supply made available to us through Christ Jesus. He did not say that Jesus would only meet spiritual needs, physical needs, or financial and material needs. Paul wrote that Jesus meets *all* manner and type of need.

🕮 Think about your life as a whole, list some of the needs that you have today—physical, emotional, relational, financial, material, spiritual.

If a person is truly honest with himself, he will admit that the things he desires most in life are the intangibles that cannot be purchased and are not man-made: health, loving relationships, fulfillment and meaning in life. Jesus Christ is ultimately the number one Source for all things that matter the most to us:

🕮 Wisdom and understanding
🕮 Total health—spirit, mind, and body
🕮 Feelings of belonging and loving relationships with others
🕮 Fulfilling and meaningful ministry to others

- Blessings that are material, emotional, and spiritual
- Hope, peace, joy, and unconditional love
- Spiritual insights and intimacy with God the Father
- Healthy self-esteem and a feeling of worthiness in knowing we are a beloved child of God
- Deliverance from evil
- Forgiveness of sin
- Freedom from guilt and shame

It is when we recognize that Christ Jesus living in us makes all things possible for us that we are able to say with the apostle Paul,

> I have learned in whatever state I am, to be content: I know how to be abased, and I know how to abound. Everywhere and in all things I have learned both to be full and to be hungry, both to abound and to suffer need. I can do all things through Christ who strengthens me.

> —Phil. 4:11–13

As long as we are relying on ourselves or on any source other than Christ to be our provision and our security, we will not be content. Why? Because deep inside we know that all man-made systems, including our own self-efforts, ultimately fall short or fail. Beauty fades, status changes, fame slides away, power wanes, possessions rust and rot. Only what Christ provides is lasting and sure. Why? Because He is eternal and trustworthy. Nobody can supply our needs as Jesus Christ can supply them!

> I also, after I heard of your faith in the Lord Jesus and your love for all the saints, do not cease to give thanks for you, making mention of you in my prayers: that the God of our Lord Jesus Christ, the Father of glory, may give to you the spirit of

wisdom and revelation in the knowledge of Him, the eyes of your understanding being enlightened; that you may know what is the hope of His calling, what are the riches of the glory of His inheritance in the saints.

—Eph. 1:15–18

☙ What is "the hope of His calling"? The "riches of the glory of His inheritance"?

☙ What is "the spirit of wisdom and revelation"? How are these attained, according to these verses?

A Fresh and Constant Supply

What Jesus gives to us is always fresh and individually designed. He never gives a stale, secondhand, or warmed-over blessing. His riches are unlimited—His storehouse is infinite and His mercy toward us daily, vibrant, life-giving, and steadfast in its supply. And we never outgrow our neediness. We never become so mature physically, emotionally, or spiritually that we no longer have needs. Just as we have a need for food, water, and fresh air on a daily basis, so we have a constant, ever-present need for God's love, care, comfort, forgiveness, mercy, and security. Jesus knows that every person has a constant need for those things that only He can give. That's why He taught His disciples,

> I am the vine, you are the branches. He who abides in Me, and I in him, bears much fruit; for without Me you can do nothing . . . If you abide in Me, and My words abide in you, you will ask what you desire, and it shall be done for you. By this My Father is glorified, that you bear much fruit; so you will be My disciples. As the Father loved Me, I also have loved you; abide in My love.

> —John 15:5, 7–9

What does it mean to abide in Christ?

60

What does it mean to have Christ's words abide in you? How is this done?

When have you seen Him keep this promise in your own life?

Why Needs Aren't Met

There are many reasons why our needs aren't met as quickly or in the way we desire. Perhaps the foremost reason is that we do not truly trust Jesus Christ to meet our needs in His way, in His timing, and according to His purposes. As James wrote, "You do not have because you do not ask" (James 4:2). Do not let your pride, ego, arrogance, or concern about pomp and prestige keep you from humbly asking God for what you need.

Furthermore, when we ask, we are to ask with faith:

> But let him ask in faith, with no doubting, for he who doubts is like a wave of the sea driven and tossed by the wind. For let not that man suppose that he will receive anything from the Lord; he is a double–minded man, unstable in all his ways.

> —James 1:6–8

Two other factors often keep us from receiving what we need:

1. Sin. We willfully choose to do things our way rather than God's way; we follow our own law rather than follow God's commandments.
2. Misplaced Motives. We desire things that are not pleasing to God or we desire to manipulate others.

God is under no obligation to answer requests that are contrary to His plan and purpose for our lives. He will not contribute to our sin, our desire to manipulate other people, or our desires that are rooted in self-pride.

🙠 Can you think of an example of "misplaced motives" in your life?

🙠 When have you willfully chosen to do things your own way? What was the result?

Covetousness and Greed

Greediness and covetousness can easily include our desire for things we think we need. Always ask yourself, "Is this something that *God* desires for me to have?" We are wise to ask only for those things that are for our eternal good and for the benefit of others around us.

His Supply Is Abundant

Jesus said, "I have come that they may have life, and that they may have it more abundantly" (John 10:10). God is not stingy. He does not supply the needs of His beloved children with meagerness. His love and mercy and provision are overflowing.

When the Lord revealed Himself to Moses, He made a statement to Moses about His own character and nature:

> And the LORD passed before him and proclaimed, "The LORD, the LORD God, merciful and gracious, longsuffering, and *abounding in goodness and truth*, keeping mercy for thousands, forgiving iniquity and transgression and sin."
>
> —Ex. 34:6, 7 (emphasis added)

There is no end to the goodness that God desires to pour out on you as His beloved child. As you grow in your obedience to Him, you will experience an increasing supply of His blessing. Out of His infinite supply, He pours an infinite blessing!

How do you feel about God's ability and desire to supply all your needs with a fresh and overflowing supply?

Define the following, giving examples of each:

Iniquity:

Transgression:

Sin:

Our Response to His Provision

Our response to the totally sufficient provision made available through Christ Jesus should be one of thanksgiving and praise. Paul wrote to the Colossians,

> As you therefore have received Christ Jesus the Lord, so walk in Him, rooted and built up in Him and established in the faith, as you have been taught, abounding in it with thanksgiving.
>
> —Col. 2:6, 7

We are to be thankful and to praise the Lord *not only when all of our need is met* but also when we are experiencing lack, knowing that Jesus Christ has met, is meeting, and will meet all of our need. No need we ever have is a surprise to Jesus Christ. He has known everything we will need to fulfill our purpose in life from the moment we were created, and along with our creation, Jesus Christ created the full provision for the meeting of all our needs. Therefore, we can thank and praise the Lord for meeting our needs, even if we don't yet see or experience the reality of His provision. As the writer to the Hebrews stated so well, "Now faith is the substance of things hoped for, the evidence of things not seen" (Heb. 11:1).

> Now may He who supplies seed to the sower, and bread for food, supply and multiply the seed you have sown and increase the fruits of your righteousness, while you are enriched in everything for all liberality, which causes thanksgiving through us to God. For the administration of this service not only supplies the needs of the saints, but also is abounding through many thanksgivings to God.
>
> 2 Cor. 9:10–12

What needs can you thank God for meeting, even though you haven't yet seen Him do it?

What role does faith play in thanking God for that which is "hoped for" and "not seen"? What is that faith based on?

❧ Today and Tomorrow ❧

TODAY: THE PROPER RESPONSE TO GOD'S SUFFICIENCY IS ALWAYS PRAISE AND THANKSGIVING.

TOMORROW: I WILL TRUST GOD TO TRANSFORM AND RENEW MY MIND.

❧ Notes and Prayer Requests: ❧

All We Need for Our Identity and Perfection

---- *In This Lesson* ----

LEARNING: IS IT POSSIBLE TO BE A PERFECT CHRISTIAN?

GROWING: WHAT IS MY ROLE IN BEING CONFORMED TO CHRIST?

So many people in our world today are struggling to define who they are, to succeed at their own self-imposed goals. They are attempting to achieve success totally in their own efforts. In some cases, people are using others to try to achieve success they desire. The Bible teaches us, however, that it is God who defines us and perfects us. It is God who has a plan for us, as the prophet Jeremiah declared: "For I know the thoughts that I think toward you, says the LORD, thoughts of peace and not of evil, to give you a future and a hope" (Jer. 29:11).

The Lord created each of us with a future! He had a good plan and purpose in mind at the instant of our creation. And, as we rely on His sufficiency, He will work diligently, tirelessly, and constantly to bring that plan and purpose to full fruition!

No More Self-Striving

For years, I felt as if I were on something of a spiritual and emotional roller coaster in my relationship with the Lord. Then I faced the fact that my problem was not created by the Lord, but by *me*. I was trying to make my own joy, my own peace, my own fulfillment, my own success, my own sense of well-being. I was striving to do what no person can do—create inner health and wholeness. When I came face-to-face with the great truth that the apostle Paul proclaims again and again in his letters—"Christ in me, I in Christ"—I found a new freedom and genuine joy in my relationship with Jesus Christ that was far beyond anything I had ever experienced.

The "Christ in me" aspect of our Christian life is what qualifies and prepares us for an eternal life in heaven. As the apostle Paul wrote to the Colossians, "Christ in you, the hope of glory" (Col. 1:27). The "I in Christ" aspect of our Christian life is what qualifies and prepares us to live a victorious life of purpose on this earth. Paul wrote to the Corinthians: "He who establishes us with you *in Christ* and has anointed us is God" (2 Cor. 1:21, emphasis added).

It is a great spiritual mystery that Christ Jesus dwells within us and we within Him. Paul readily admits that to the Colossians, saying, "To them God willed to make known what are the riches of the glory of this mystery among the Gentiles" (Col. 1:27). This truth about our relationship with Christ cannot be understood totally with the rational mind. Those who are not Christians *cannot* understand the relationship a believer has with Christ, and we should never expect a nonbeliever to be able to understand this mystery with his mind. It is a spiritual truth that is understood only from the perspective of faith, or "believing." It is on the basis of our believing that Christ indwells us and we dwell in Him.

Christ dwelling within us becomes our *identity*, and it is His presence within us that leads to our *perfection*. We no longer belong to ourselves. We no longer are responsible for fashioning ourselves or making ourselves. We are under Christ's authority, we are His responsibility, we are totally subject to His will. He lives His life through us, and in the process, He transforms us and builds us up so that we feel tremendous joy, satisfaction, and fulfillment.

The Christian life is not a life of self-effort, but rather, it is allowing Jesus to live through us. Consider the difference between an artesian well and a pump. A pump requires effort and energy to pull the water up from the earth. In an artesian well or natural fountain, the water bubbles up of its own accord. No effort on the part of man is required. In like manner, when we trust Jesus Christ to be sufficient for all things in our lives, His Spirit bubbles up in us like a river of living water (see John 7:37–39). We do not need to strive to work up our faith; rather, we let His presence fill us and flow through us.

In your life, have you had experiences or times when you truly allowed the Holy Spirit to move through you to minister to others?

Conformed to Christ

Paul wrote to the Romans of the plan of God for every believer, saying,

> For whom He foreknew, he also predestined to be conformed
> to the image of His Son, that He might be the firstborn among
> many brethren. Moreover whom He predestined, these He also
> called; whom He called, these He also justified; and whom He
> justified, these He also glorified. (Rom. 8:29, 30)

You are in process! So is every other believer in Christ. We are not in-
stantly made perfect when we accept Jesus Christ as our Savior. As the
familiar bumper sticker says, "Christians aren't perfect, just forgiven."
It is *as* we continue to put our trust in Jesus Christ to be the Lord of our
lives that He does a perfecting, refining, work in us. The terms Paul uses
are *conform* and *justifies*. "To conform" means to fashion something
so that it is in exact likeness to a pattern. Jesus is the pattern. The Holy
Spirit is making us so that we are *like* Jesus in our attitude, our reliance
upon God the Father, our mercy, love, words, and behavior.

One of the meanings of the word *justify* is to "line up." When a printer
justifies type, he lines up the type so that the left margin is even and the
right margin is even—as we see in most newspaper columns. When we
accept Jesus as our Savior, God embarks upon a process of lining us up
with the character and nature of Christ, making us more and more like
Jesus every day for the rest of our lives. The Holy Spirit operates as the
agent of re-creation and transformation in our lives. He is the One who
molds us into the person God designed us to be.

The end result of our justification is our glorification—the more we are
like Jesus Christ, the more we bring glory to Him and the greater His
glory is revealed through us. The perfecting process brings us into genuine conformity to the nature and spiritual likeness of Christ.

The Lord will perfect that which concerns me; Your mercy, O Lord, endures forever; Do not forsake the works of Your hands.

—Ps. 138:8

What does the Psalmist mean by "The Lord will perfect that which concerns me"?

How do you see God's perfecting work being accomplished in you?

Perfection Involves a Breaking Process

A breaking process is sometimes required for us to be perfected. Too often we look at the difficult times in our lives and ask, "Where is God? Why doesn't God do something about this circumstance or situation?" The fact is, God is present and He *is* doing something! The better questions to ask are these: "*What* is it, Lord, that You are trying to teach me through this? *What* is it that You are trying to change in me?"

☙ In your life, have you ever had an experience in which you felt the Lord was breaking you in order to bring about a positive change?

Perfection Involves a Transformation in Our

Thinking

As we are conformed to Jesus Christ, we begin to desire more and more to be like Him—to feel what He felt for other people, to love as He loved, to think what He thought, and to apply Scripture as He applied it. The more we seek to think the very thoughts of Jesus, the more our minds are renewed by the Holy Spirit. We have a new and increasingly great

74

ability to understand the Bible when we read it. We have new insights into what God is doing in our lives, in the lives of others, and in the world as a whole. Paul wrote to the Romans,

> And do not be conformed to this world, but be transformed by the renewing of your mind, that you may prove what is that good and acceptable and perfect will of God.

—Rom. 12:2

The transformation of our minds means that over time, we have a different worldview. We see things from God's point of view. We desire only to know and to do God's will because we have a new understanding that God's truth is lasting and eternally beneficial.

What does it mean to be "conformed to this world"? To be "transformed"?

⮞ What does it mean to renew your mind? How is this done? Why is it vitally important?

Perfection Involves a "Putting Off and Putting On"

Process

Paul described this remaking process to the Colossians in this way: Some aspects of our nature we are to "put off"—just as we would take off dirty, tattered clothing, and other aspects of Christ's nature we are to "put on." He encouraged the Colossians, "Set your mind on things above, not on things on the earth" (Col. 3:2). He then went on to write,

But now you yourselves are to put off all these: anger, wrath, malice, blasphemy, filthy language out of your mouth. Do not lie to one another, since you have put off the old man with his deeds, and have put on the new man who is renewed in knowledge according to the image of Him who created him . . .

Therefore, as the elect of God, holy and beloved, put on tender mercies, kindness, humility, meekness, longsuffering; bearing with one another, and forgiving one another, if anyone has a complaint against another; even as Christ forgave you, so you also must do. But above all these things put on love, which is the bond of perfection.

—Col. 3:8–10, 12–14

Our part, through an act of our will and as an expression of our faith, is to *choose* not to engage in sinful behaviors and to *choose* instead to pursue righteous attitudes and behaviors. We do the choosing, and then the Holy Spirit gives us both the courage and the ability to follow through and act on our decisions. The Holy Spirit empowers us to obey once we have made our choice to obey God.

Perfection Involves a Building-Up Process

The perfection process in us is not only a breaking and remaking process, but a process of building up. Those parts of us that are in need of remaking, the Lord breaks. Those aspects of our lives that are good in God's sight are the aspects that the Lord strengthens, fortifies, and builds up. The Holy Spirit is the *Master of edification,* which is a term the Bible uses for the building up of a person's character and spirit. A firm, well-laid foundation is essential for a building to be strong—our foundation is Jesus Christ and the Word of God. Alignment of all aspects of a building is necessary for the building to be strong—the Cornerstone of our faith, Jesus Christ, enables us to come into proper alignment and to be fitted together well.

The building-up process always involves our relationships with others. We are never made perfect in a vacuum. God always uses other people as instruments to sand away and chisel our flaws, to teach us and counsel us with wisdom, and to build us up emotionally. God is not only giving you an identity as a person, but He is also putting you into a fellowship of believers so that, with others, you have an identity as His body. Your faith does not exist or operate apart from others; you are part of a church as a whole.

≈ In your life, can you cite instances or ways in which the Holy Spirit has helped you to increase or strengthen your natural God-given abilities and talents?

🐾 How has the Lord used other people to bring about your identity and your perfection in Christ Jesus?

🐾 Today and Tomorrow 🐾

TODAY: BEING CONFORMED TO CHRIST IS A PROCESS GOD IS WORKING IN ME EVERY DAY.

TOMORROW: I WILL TURN TO THE BIBLE WHEN I AM CHALLENGED BY THE VIEWS OF THE WORLD.

❧ Notes and Prayer Requests: ❧

All We Need to Have Meaning for Our Lives

❧ In This Lesson ☙

LEARNING: WHAT OUTSIDE SOURCES ARE INFLUENCING ME TO BELIEVE FALSE VIEWS OF GOD?

GROWING: WHAT DOES THE BIBLE HAVE TO SAY REGARDING THESE VIEWS?

The Greek culture in which many of the first-century Christians lived was a world very much like the one in which we live. People were greatly concerned with the meaning of life. Lengthy discussions and debates focused on the age-old questions, "Who am I? Why am I here? What is life all about? Where does it all end?" The apostle Paul addressed these concerns in his letter to the Colossians:

> Beware lest anyone cheat you through philosophy and empty deceit, according to the tradition of men, according to the basic principles of the world, and not according to Christ. For in Him dwells all the fullness of the Godhead bodily; and you are complete in Him, who is the head of all principality and power.

> —Col. 2:8–10

First, Paul says that he does not want the Colossians to be cheated by the world's philosophy. This word is translated in some versions of the Bible as "captured"—in the Greek language the term is actually two words that literally mean "taken away as booty" and in the process, being "deprived of freedom." Paul does not want the Colossians to become slaves to the world or prisoners of Satan because they have been enticed to believe the wrong things. He does not want them to be cheated of genuine spiritual freedom.

🕮 Have you ever been held back, kept in a type of bondage, or hindered in your walk with Christ by an error in your thinking?

Your Spiritual Freedom Can Be Taken from You

Paul warned that we can be cheated of our spiritual freedom if we buy into the philosophy of the world. Philosophy is concerned with three main things:

1. The existence of man, which leads us to ask, "Who am I?"
2. The source of all things, which leads us to ask, "Where did I come from?"
3. The purpose of all things, which leads us to ask, "Why am I here?"

Every religion on earth attempts to answer these philosophical questions in some way, and often very elaborately. Paul admonished the Colossians not to be caught up in vast systems of philosophical belief, but rather, to stick with the simplicity of the gospel:

1. You are a beloved child of God, made in His image.
2. You are a creation of God, born again by the power of the Holy Spirit at work in your life.
3. You were destined by God from your creation to be conformed to the image of Christ and to fulfill God's unique plan and purpose for you on this earth.

As for the end of all things, the Bible teaches plainly that God gives everlasting life to those who believe in Jesus Christ (see John 3:16) and that He will reward all believers for what they do to further the kingdom of God on this earth. But how often do we find people who try to make the truth of God more complicated than this? They add long lists of things a person must do to find meaning in life and to attain a good life in the world to come. They add to the gospel, and then add more to the gospel, and then add more to the gospel, until very often the gospel has all but disappeared from their teaching.

In the case of false religions, the performance of rituals is put in place of faith in the gospel. Those who deny the gospel and propose something in its place are guilty of "empty deceit." What they proclaim leads to nothing and has no bearing on eternal life. It may sound good. It may even produce a warm emotional feeling. But in the end, the teaching has no consequence for good, no lasting fruit. What such teachers teach is actually a lie that detracts and leads a person away from the truth. Paul says about the philosophy and empty deceit: Don't be cheated! Don't be captured!

🙊 In your life, have you ever been led astray by those who would seek to add something to the gospel, or replace the gospel with another system of belief?

🙊 Put the following into your own words, then consider how each might influence your life this week:

Beloved child of God:

Created and born again:

Becoming conformed to the image of Christ:

Avoiding the False Traditions of Men

Paul also warned the Colossians against "the tradition of men, according to the basic principles of the world" (2:8). At the time Paul was writing, four main streams of thought were prevalent among both the Gentiles and the Greek-influenced Jews:

1. Legalism, a strict by-the-book approach to the code of law with little concern for the biblical "spirit of the law." Jesus referred to this legalism as "the tradition of the elders." The Law of Moses was no longer considered sufficient, but rather, an elaborate system of laws that interpreted the Law of Moses was called the law. These laws determined, for example, how far a person could travel on the Sabbath and how certain rituals were to be performed. Nearly seven hundred of these ritualistic laws were in effect at the time of Jesus.

2. Asceticism, which often took the form of self-denial. Much value was seen to be derived from fasting and withdrawing from the world so that one's senses could be sharpened and one's appreciation for the finer things in life could be refined. The Greeks regarded beauty as a very high ideal.

3. Mysticism, which was a concern for all things that were ethereal and unknown. For example, pagan Greeks often sought information from oracles, who usually functioned in a drug-induced trance and in a cloud of incense that was also laced with drugs.

4. Hedonism, which was the Greek belief that the spirit was of supreme importance and the body was simply to be used by man. From one perspective, the body was to be subjected into strict discipline so that the spirit of man might more effectively function and be more clearly reflected to others. From a near opposite perspective, the body could also be abused through excessive drinking, gluttony, and numerous sexual encounters because in the end, the body was of little importance.

℞ In your life, can you see areas in which you may have been influenced toward one or more of these ways of thinking?

Legalism—

Asceticism—

Mysticism—

Hedonism—

℞ What were the results?

What are some of the ways these four streams of thought are manifested in our world today? Consider the following statements that are heard often but are directly opposed to the gospel:

1. Legalism. "You have to know the rules of the game if you are going to be a winner." "If you don't keep all of God's rules, God is going to judge you." "If you break too many of God's rules or break them too often, you lose your chance of being forgiven." Jesus taught, "Unless one is born again, he cannot see the kingdom of God . . . You must be born again" (John 3:3, 7).

2. Asceticism. "I have to work out two hours a day and keep my body in tip-top shape if I'm going to succeed in this life." "The clothes make the man." "Being beautiful is more important than being smart." "Success is the best revenge." Jesus taught,

> Blessed are the poor in spirit, for theirs is the kingdom of heaven. Blessed are those who mourn, for they shall be comforted. Blessed are the meek, for they shall inherit the earth. Blessed are those who hunger and thirst for righteousness, for they shall be filled.
>
> —Matt. 5:3–6

3. Mysticism. "It's not wrong to dabble in various New Age practices because these things can make me more spiritual." "All religions are equal, so it's good to try various ones to see which ones work for you." But "Jesus said to him, 'I am the way, the truth, and the life. No one comes to the Father except through Me'" (John 14:6).

4. Hedonism. "If it feels good, do it?" "Try it, you'll like it." "Eat, drink, and be merry." "If you can't afford it, charge it." Jesus taught, "Let your light so shine before men, that they may see your good works and glorify your Father in heaven" (Matt. 5:16). We are not to live for our own pleasure, but rather, to give pleasure to God through loving service and a pure witness to others.

Turning Away from the "Principles of the World"

What are the principles of the world? Four of the main principles by which the world systems operate are these:

1. Man is sufficient unto himself. In other words, man is an end unto himself. The world proclaims that man has the ability to decide within himself what to think and how to act, and that no redemption of man is necessary since man can determine his own fate through acts of his will alone.

2. Today is all that matters. The world is very now-focused—we live in a society that demands instant gratification and immediate rewards. While Jesus certainly taught us to live in the present moment, trusting God for every hour of our lives, He also taught that we are to recognize that our faith and our actions have eternal consequences.

3. Happiness can be bought. It can be generated by the possession or use of things, including alcohol, drugs, and other substances taken into the body.

4. Fate determines many things in life. Stress, for example, is blamed for causing many things when in many cases, misplaced priorities and sin—both of which are subject to human will and human choices—are at the root of the problem. To believe in fate is to deny the omnipotence and omniscience of God. It is to say that there are moments in one's life in which God is not involved, does not know what is happening, or is not in control. Many people turn to astrology and horoscopes believing that they can find a clue there as to what will lie ahead for them on any given day; the Bible calls such practices idolatry because they put one's reliance on fate rather than on trusting God.

≈ In your life, have you ever felt yourself giving in to these four principles of the world?

≈ Which of these four worldly principles are you most prone to embrace? Why? How can you avoid this lie in the future?

Many Christians find themselves victims to these worldly principles. Some live as if the weight of the world has fallen on their shoulders. They are burdened and frustrated by all the responsibilities they have— they vacillate between the aspirin bottle and antacid tablets to relieve their headaches and their upset stomachs. Other Christians look for their faith to pay instant rewards—if they don't receive from God what they desire immediately, they begin to doubt God or turn away from God. Still others look to external things to generate their happiness or to dictate what happens to them in a day.

Again, Paul's response to these worldly principles would be: Don't be cheated! Don't be taken captive! Instead, take the full truth of God's Word into your mind and live it day by day, regardless of circumstances and temporary setbacks.

Key Questions We Must Ask Ourselves

You may need to know certain facts, formulas, principles, or procedures as you make your way through this material world, but the only opinions and truth that you need for your eternal soul—both now and forever—are to be found in God's Word.

"Are you saying that the only book I should be reading is the Bible?" you might ask. No . . . what I am saying is that when it comes to truth you stake your life on, when it comes to what you believe, when it comes to the foundation for your faith, when it comes to where you turn for meaning that is deep, abiding, and eternal, you must turn to God's Word! No substitute will do. And furthermore, nothing other than the Word of God is required. Jesus Christ in you—and as His words abide in you—is your total Sufficiency for truth, meaning, and value in life. What He says is all that counts when it comes to your being born again, your relationship with God, and your eternal destiny.

There are three things you must ask of your own thinking and believing, as well as about any opinion you encounter or any philosophy that may be taught to you:

1. What am I believing that does not line up with the Word of God?
2. What habits do I have that do not line up with the Word of God?
3. Is this teaching or opinion of God or is it of man? Does it line up with the truth of God's Word?

❧ Today and Tomorrow ❧

TODAY: WHEN IT COMES TO WHERE I TURN FOR MEANING THAT IS DEEP, ABIDING, AND ETERNAL, I MUST TURN TO GOD'S WORD.

TOMORROW: I WILL RELY ON JESUS CHRIST TO DIRECT ME INTO THE MINISTRY THAT HE WANTS ME TO PURSUE.

∞ **Notes and Prayer Requests:** ∞

All We Need for a Vibrant Life in the Church

❧ In This Lesson ❧

LEARNING: WHAT PART DOES THE BODY OF CHRIST PLAY IN MY LIFE?

GROWING: WHAT PART DO I PLAY IN THE BODY OF CHRIST?

As a pastor, I have come to recognize these categories of people who attend a church: those who are *active* in the life of the church; those who sit on the periphery and for the most part are *passive*—they may attend church and occasionally put something in the offering plate, but they leave the minute the service is over and are not involved in church activities or outreach; and those who drift away over time and are *inactive*—they may attend church on Christmas Eve and Easter Sunday but for the most part, they never enter the door of a church.

Why do people become passive or inactive when it comes to their life in the church? I believe the two main reasons are these: 1) They get entangled in sin of some type and they don't want to confess or repent of that sin; and 2) they don't really understand what they joined when they became a church member. Many people join churches thinking they have aligned themselves with some type of religious organization, which might give them greater social status or good business contacts. If that is their motivation, they can readily become disillusioned with various church members or practices, lose interest, or move on to another organization that they hope will meet their needs for belonging and worthiness.

The apostle Paul addressed the issue of the church in his letter to the Colossians, stating about Christ Jesus,

> He is the head of the body, the church, who is the beginning, the firstborn from the dead, that in all things He may have the preeminence.

—Col. 1:18

What does it truly mean for Jesus Christ to be the head of the church? That is the focus for this lesson.

❧ What does each of the following mean, in your own words?

Head of the body:

The firstborn from the dead:

He must have preeminence:

↘ Why are these doctrines important to the correct functioning of the church?

Christ Jesus Is the Head of the Church

The Greek term for *church* literally means "called out of"—the first-century Christians perceived that they had been called out of the world and set apart for God's purposes. They saw themselves as a body of believers under the leadership, or headship, of Jesus Christ. The word for *church* is used in three distinct ways in the New Testament:

1. The body of all believers—all saved people—of all ages. A person becomes a part of this body through belief in the blood

of Jesus Christ as the atonement necessary to bring about reconciliation with God and to experience forgiveness from sin by
God's grace. The universal body of believers includes all people
who declare Jesus Christ to be Savior and Lord.

2. Believers in a specific locality, place, or city. The Colossians
were the believers in the city of Colosse. In writing to these
believers, Paul said that his letter should be "read also in the
church of the Laodiceans" (Col. 4:16).

*3. Believers in one specific group of people who met together to
worship God.* In writing to the Colossians, Paul said: "Greet the
brethren who are in Laodicea, and Nymphas and the church that
is in his house" (Col. 4:15).

The most prevalent meaning for the term *church* is the first—the universal body of all believers. The church is not a building or a denomination.
It is *all* Christians *everywhere*. When a person believes in Jesus Christ
as his or her Savior and seeks to identify with and follow Jesus Christ
as Lord, that person is automatically a part of the universal church, regardless of other affiliations he or she may have.

☙ In your life, have you had experiences in local, area-wide, and
the "universal" church . . . based solely on your belief in Jesus
Christ apart from any type of organizational membership?

Jesus Christ is the founder of the church; He is its *only* founder. In Matthew 16, Jesus asked His disciples what others were saying about Him. He then asked the disciples directly, "But who do you say that I am?" Simon Peter answered and said, "You are the Christ, the Son of the living God." Jesus responded to Peter this way:

> Blessed are you, Simon Bar-Jonah, for flesh and blood has not revealed this to you, but My Father who is in heaven. And I also say to you that you are Peter, and on this rock I will build My church, and the gates of Hades shall not prevail against it.

> —Matt. 16:17, 18

On the basis of this passage of Scripture, there are those who say that Peter was the founder of the church. Jesus, however, was not building the church on Peter, but rather on the truth of the statement that Peter made: Jesus is the Christ, the Son of the living God. It is those who believe this truth who are genuine *church* members.

Why is it so important for us to recognize what the church is and who the founder of the church is?

Jesus Christ is both the way a person enters the church and He is the One who causes the church to exist, to function, to prosper and grow, and to be used to extend His kingdom on this earth. You can have a social club, an organization, and even a religious group without Jesus Christ . . . but you cannot have a genuine church without Jesus Christ as its founder, head, and ongoing source of spiritual life. You can meet with a group of people to follow a ritual or sing songs or hear lectures . . . but you cannot truly function as a church unless Jesus Christ is central to all that you do. He is the Sufficiency for the church; indeed, He alone is the Creator and the Sustainer of His church.

Errors We Make About the Church

We make a grave mistake any time we think the church is:

❦ *Limited to a particular denomination.* Denominations were never God's intention or design. Denominations formed on the basis of doctrine (beliefs) and policy (organization). They often reflect different approaches to styles of worship and different cultural backgrounds. The church as a whole includes people from many denominations who truly believe that Jesus is the Christ.

❦ *Any religious group that calls itself a church.* A number of cults exist today that deny the deity of Christ Jesus and yet still claim to be a "church." The plain and simple fact is that if Jesus Christ is not regarded as the Son of God and if He isn't the head, the "body" isn't a church!

❦ *Something that we can join apart from an active faith in Jesus Christ and a reliance upon Him as our Savior.* Signing the membership roll of a church does not make a person a Christian. Baptism as an infant does not result in the conversion of the human heart. Going through various church rituals by rote because a person reaches a particular age or finishes a particular class does not make a person a member of the body of Christ. Only those who, with their wills, accept Jesus Christ as the substitutionary, definitive, and only necessary sacrifice for their sin, and who believe in Jesus Christ as Savior can be members of the church.

What affects have you observed from these false beliefs about the church?

Why is each of these three principles important to a correct understanding of the church? What happens when any of them is not followed?

A Matter of "Dead or Alive"

The real issue associated with your being a part of the church—Christ's own body—is not whether you are an active member, a passive member, or an inactive member. It is much more serious than that. Membership in an organization may have degrees of activity. Being part of an organism is something else entirely. It is a matter of *life and death spiritually*.

When one part of the body dies, it often turns gangrenous and the result will be death unless that dead tissue is removed. When one part of a body dies, the entire body suffers. This is also true in the church. Jesus Christ *is* the life of the church. It is His life that flows into each member of the church, great or small. It is His life that gives life, vibrancy, purpose, meaning, fulfillment, and energy to each member and to the whole. Paul wrote this very plainly to the Colossians: "When Christ *who is our life* appears, then you also will appear with Him in glory" (Col. 3:4, emphasis added). Without Him, you are spiritually dead. With Him, you are alive.

How alive are you? Is your spirit vibrantly alive today, or just barely alive?

When you accepted Jesus Christ as your Savior, you became a part of His living body. You became a branch in the living vine of Christ (see John 15:1–8). The eternal life source of the Holy Spirit began to course through every facet of your being—spirit, mind, emotions, and body.

If a person chooses to withdraw from Christ, to pursue sin, or in any way seeks to diminish the work of the Holy Spirit in his life, he slows down the pumping of the life source of the Holy Spirit into his life and through his life to others. He clogs the vessel of his own life. He becomes less effective, less energized by the Spirit, less healthy and whole spiritually, emotionally, and rationally. His inner self begins to atrophy, just as a muscle withers and becomes ineffective if the flow of energy through the nervous system and the blood vessels is constricted or limited.

The Lord gave a very sharp warning to the Laodicean church about the state of their spiritual life:

> I know your works, that you are neither cold nor hot. I could wish you were cold or hot. So then, because you are lukewarm, and neither cold nor hot, I will vomit you out of My mouth. Because you say, "I am rich, have become wealthy, and have need of nothing"—and do not know that you are wretched miserable, poor, blind, and naked . . . As many as I love, I rebuke and chasten. Therefore be zealous and repent.
>
> —Rev. 3:15–17, 19

🔊 How does Jesus' rebuke and chastening reflect His love?

 Do you identify at all with the church in Laodicea?

He Is the One Who Makes Our Ministry Effective

What does it mean for us to rely on Christ Jesus for our spiritual life
and vibrancy—both individually and as a group of believers?

*1. It means we rely totally on Jesus Christ to direct us into the ministry
avenues that He wants us to pursue.* Paul wrote,

> For we are God's fellow workers; you are God's field, you are
> God's building. According to the grace of God which was given
> to me, as a wise master builder I have laid the foundation, and
> another builds on it . . . If anyone's work which he has built on
> it endures, he will receive a reward.

> —1 Cor. 3:9, 10, 14

Ask yourself continually:

    ✎ Am I ministering to others in the way that Jesus Christ desires for me to minister?

    ✎ Am I involved in the ministry projects that the Lord desires for me to do? Or, am I doing various things for my personal glorification or simply because I didn't have the courage to say no?

    ✎ Am I listening continually for the Lord's direction so that I will be flexible and quick to act as He leads and guides me?

2. It means that we rely totally on Jesus Christ to make us effective. We each must do our part—using our gifts and our talents fully—but in the end, we must trust Jesus Christ to do what none of us can do. Only He can save souls, deliver from evil, and make people whole. Paul wrote clearly to the Corinthians,

> Who then is Paul, and who is Apollos, but ministers through whom you believed, as the Lord gave to each one? I planted, Apollos watered, but God gave the increase. So then neither he who plants is anything, nor he who waters, but God who gives the increase. Now he who plants and he who waters are one, and each one will receive his own reward according to his own labor.

> —1 Cor. 3:5–8

Are you truly trusting God to work through you to others? Never discount what you do in the name of Jesus. Do not be reluctant to serve others because you think you can do so little or know so little. Give to Jesus what you *do* have and watch Him multiply it and use it to bless others. After all, He multiplied a little boy's lunch of five loaves and two fish (see Mark 6:37–44). What might the Lord do with what *you* give Him!

❧ Today and Tomorrow ❧

TODAY: THE CHURCH IS A LIVING ORGANISM, NOT AN ORGANIZATION. IT IS ALIVE AND SPIRITUAL. IT IS THE BODY OF CHRIST.

TOMORROW: I WILL COMMIT MYSELF TO SEEKING THE TRUTH OF GOD.

Accessing the Sufficiency of Jesus Christ

❧ In This Lesson ☙

LEARNING: WHAT DOES IT MEAN THAT JESUS IS SUFFICIENT FOR ALL MY NEEDS?

GROWING: HOW DO I TAP INTO THIS ALL-SUFFICIENCY?

How do we access the sufficiency of Christ Jesus? How do we tap into His effectiveness and the richness of His character? How do we become saved, victorious, confident Christians who trust Him completely and live in His sufficiency?

The process is threefold:

1. We must *commit* ourselves to seeking the truth of God, which includes the truth of Jesus Christ's sufficiency to meet all of our needs. We must desire to know the truth of God's Word and to apply His truth to our lives.
2. We must *confess* the truth of God, and especially confess that the truth of God pertains to our personal lives.
3. We must *claim* the truth of God for our lives by our faith.

Commit to the Truth

The psalmist made a tremendous statement about the truth we find in God's Word:

> The law of the LORD is perfect, converting the soul; the testimony of the LORD is sure, making wise the simple; the statutes of the LORD are right, rejoicing the heart; the commandment of the LORD is pure, enlightening the eyes; the fear of the LORD is clean, enduring forever; the judgments of the LORD are true and righteous altogether. More to be desired are they than gold, yea, than much fine gold; sweeter also than honey and the honeycomb. Moreover by them Your servant is warned. And in keeping them there is great reward.
>
> —Ps. 19:7–11

The truth does not come to us automatically. We must search it out. We must be diligent in our reading and study of God's Word so that we truly know God's opinion, God's desires, God's commandments. We must *pursue* the truth. And when we find it and follow it, we find that we experience great blessing!

How do you pursue the truth for each aspect of your life?

≈ Define each of the following, and show how each is different from the others:

The law of the LORD:

The testimony of the LORD:

The statutes of the LORD:

The commandment of the LORD:

The fear of the LORD:

The judgments of the LORD:

Confess the Truth

Tremendous power is released when we confess the truth of God to ourselves and to others. To confess is to openly and directly state something. Repeatedly throughout Scripture, we find that the visible world was created by the invisible Word of God. Read the passage of Genesis 1 below. Note each time you find the phrase "God said."

Then God said, "Let there be light"; and there was light. And God saw the light, that it was good; and God divided the light from the darkness. God called the light Day, and the darkness He called Night. So the evening and the morning were the first day.

Then God said, "Let there be a firmament in the midst of the waters, and let it divide the waters from the waters." Thus God made the firmament, and divided the waters which were under the firmament from the waters which were above the firmament; and it was so. And God called the firmament Heaven. So the evening and the morning were the second day.

Then God said, "Let the waters under the heavens be gathered together into one place, and let the dry land appear"; and it was so. And God called the dry land Earth, and the gathering together of the waters He called Seas. And God saw that it was good.

Then God said, "Let the earth bring forth grass, the herb that yields seed, and the fruit tree that yields fruit according to its kind, whose seed is in itself, on the earth"; and it was so. And the earth brought forth grass, the herb that yields seed according to its kind, and the tree that yields fruit, whose seed is in itself according to its kind. And God saw that it was good. So the evening and the morning were the third day.

Then God said, "Let there be lights in the firmament of the heavens to divide the day from the night; and let them be for signs and seasons, and for days and years; and let them be for lights in the firmament of the heavens to give light on the earth"; and it was so. Then God made two great lights: the greater light to rule the day, and the lesser light to rule the night. He made the stars also. God set them in the firmament of the heavens to give light on the earth, and to rule over the day and over the night, and to divide the light from the darkness. And God saw that it was good. So the evening and the morning were the fourth day.

Then God said, "Let the waters abound with an abundance of living creatures, and let birds fly above the earth across the face of the firmament of the heavens." So God created great sea creatures and every living thing that moves, with which the waters abounded, according to their kind, and every winged bird according to its kind. And God saw that it was good. And God blessed them, saying, "Be fruitful and multiply, and fill the waters in the seas, and let birds multiply on the earth." So the evening and the morning were the fifth day.

Then God said, "Let the earth bring forth the living creature according to its kind: cattle and creeping thing and beast of the earth, each according to its kind"; and it was so. And God made the beast of the earth according to its kind, cattle according to its kind, and everything that creeps on the earth according to its kind. And God saw that it was good.

Then God said, "Let Us make man in Our image, according to Our likeness; let them have dominion over the fish of the sea, over the birds of the air, and over the cattle, over all the earth and over every creeping thing that creeps on the earth."

So God created man in His own image; in the image of God He created him; male and female He created them. Then God blessed them, and God said to them, "Be fruitful and multiply; fill the earth and subdue it; have dominion over the fish of the sea, over the birds of the air, and over every living thing that moves on the earth."

And God said, "See, I have given you every herb that yields seed which is on the face of all the earth, and every tree whose fruit yields seed; to you it shall be for food. Also, to every beast of the earth, to every bird of the air, and to everything that creeps on the earth, in which there is life, I have given every green herb for food"; and it was so. Then God saw everything that He had made, and indeed it was very good. So the evening and the morning were the sixth day.

—Gen. 1:3–31

God created, again and again, by speaking various aspects of our universe into existence. Then God defined what He had created, again by speaking His Word. Read Genesis 1 again. This time note how many times you find the phrase "God called." In naming things, God was giving them an identity, a purpose, and a definition—He was expressing the truth of His creation and how it was to function. Also note the various ways in which God gave order and limitations to the world He made.

And finally, God established and blessed what He had made, sealing the truth of His creation through His spoken word. Read Genesis 1 yet a third time. This time note how many times you find the phrase "And God saw that it was good." God was pleased with what He had made and the way in which He had made it to function, and He established it as His law forevermore. Once God made something, defined it with various laws, and established it as "good" in His sight, the thing God made was accomplished. It was true.

🐌 What new insights do you have into Genesis 1?

🐌 Why did God give things names? What does this suggest about His relationship with His creation?

What does this mean for us today? It means that God made you. He made me. He spoke each of us into existence long before we were conceived in our mothers' wombs. He "called" you—He defined you and gave you specific talents, gifts, and dreams. All your life He has continued to call you, giving you ongoing guidance, direction, relationships, and protection. God created you and God has molded you. Any work that God has done in your life is permanent—it cannot be destroyed or taken away. It is the *truth* about who you are as His beloved child and as a person who is born again and saved forever.

✎ Reflect back over your life. Identify some of the permanent things that God has done in you and for you.

❧ What does it mean to you that God knows your name? That He looks upon you as "good"?

God speaks—and in doing so, He creates the visible from the invisible. He creates a truth that is not only truth in theory, but truth in reality. Paul wrote to the Romans that it is God "who gives life to the dead and calls those things which do not exist as though they did" (Rom. 4:17).

This is also an especially important concept for you to believe when it comes to those things that you lack but are necessary for you to have full confidence and to be fully effective. Everything that Jesus Christ speaks to you about you, about Himself, and about the relationship He desires to have with you are rock-bottom truths that you can base your life upon. Jesus Christ speaks the truth to you, and when you accept His truth and believe it and then speak it to yourself and others, the truth of His Word becomes a reality in your life.

Do you need more strength or power? More wisdom?—the solution to a problem, the answer to a nagging question? More love? Look for passages in God's Word that speak about the strength and power, the all-wise nature, or the great love of the Lord. Receive those verses into your own heart and mind, knowing that it is the Lord who lives within you! And then confess or state those verses aloud to yourself. Proclaim the truth of God's Word to your own heart and mind.

It is God's invisible truth—the meaning underlying the words in your Bible—that becomes a *visible* reality in our lives when we begin to believe that truth and act on it. Everything the Bible says about you as a beloved child of God, one called to be a joint heir with Christ Jesus, is not only true, but it is irreversible. Once you have claimed any gift, trait, or promise offered to you freely and lovingly by the Lord Jesus Christ, it cannot be taken away from you.

Claiming the Truth

Those things that are promised to us by God and that we claim by our faith are what become the reality of truth inside us. In accepting Jesus as our Savior, we make a faith claim—we accept with our faith and believe that what God has said about the death of Jesus on the Cross is true. And it is as we believe and receive Jesus *by faith* that Jesus becomes our Savior and the Holy Spirit begins to reside within us. This same principle applies to everything that is promised by God to us. We must claim that we *receive* it into our lives *by our faith*.

Faith is the key to receiving and accepting the sufficiency of Christ Jesus for every area of our lives. When we desire the sufficiency of Christ to be made a reality in our lives in any area of lack or need that we are experiencing, we must *receive and believe* that God's Word is true for us, and that we are in possession of all that Christ offers to us.

A Daily Process

Committing ourselves to the pursuit of truth, confessing the truth of God as being applicable to our own lives, and claiming by our faith that we receive the truth of Christ's sufficiency for us is a threefold *ongoing process*. We cannot commit ourselves to the truth only once—it is something we must do daily, asking the Holy Spirit to lead and guide us into all truth as Jesus promised He would (see John 16:13).

Confessing the truth of God for our own lives is something that we must do daily as we read God's Word. Every portion of the Word of God is true for you and for me. It is the *way* God intends for us to think, believe, feel, respond, speak, and act. Receiving the truth of Christ's sufficiency is also something we must do daily. We must claim that Jesus *is* the Lord over every situation in our lives and that He is our all in all, in every circumstance and in the face of every need.

> So the Lord said, "If you have faith as a mustard seed, you can say to this mulberry tree, 'Be pulled up by the roots and be planted in the sea,' and it would obey you."
>
> —Luke 17:6

How big is your faith?

❧ In what ways can you trust God to grow you in your faith?

❧ Today and Tomorrow ❧

TODAY: WHEN I AM FAITHFUL IN DOING MY PART—COMMITTING MY MIND TO THE TRUTH, CONFESSING WITH MY MOUTH THE TRUTH, AND CLAIMING IN MY HEART THE TRUTH—THEN THE HOLY SPIRIT DOES HIS PART IN MY LIFE.

TOMORROW: I WILL TRUST HIM TO MEET ALL OF MY NEEDS THROUGH THE OVER-FLOWING AND GLORIOUS RICHES OF CHRIST.

Choosing to Live in His Sufficiency

As believers in Christ Jesus, we have everything we need to live a victorious life and to receive eternal life.

Spiritually, we have Jesus within.

Morally, we have the Holy Spirit available to help us make the right choices daily and to exemplify Christ to the world.

Mentally, we have the Holy Spirit as our Teacher and Counselor—One fully capable of leading us into all truth.

Physically and materially, we have access to the full riches in glory by Christ Jesus (Phil. 4:9).

Emotionally, we have Jesus as our total Sufficiency for love, relationship, wholeness, value, worthiness, and a sense of belonging.

When we say, "I need . . ." and we complete that statement with anything other than or in addition to Christ Jesus, we begin to justify our sin or develop a rationale that is based upon a lie. The truth is that we are *complete* in Christ. He has the capacity and ability to meet all of our needs.

The question is not really one of Christ's sufficiency—He is sufficient and that is an absolute truth of God—but rather, the question is whether we have made a choice to receive Christ's sufficiency into our lives. Have we made a decision with our will to know the truth, speak the truth, receive the truth, and then live by the truth that Jesus Christ is our total Sufficiency for all needs, in all circumstances, and in all aspects of life?

If you have not made that decision to allow Jesus Christ to live in you and through you *with the abundance of His sufficiency,* I invite you to make that decision today. I encourage you to pray:

> Lord Jesus, I have been prideful and arrogant. I have lived independently from You. I confess that I have sinned against You. I ask You to forgive me for my sin of unbelief and for trying to live my life my own way and according to my own limited resources. I believe Jesus Christ died on the Cross for my sins. I believe that He makes available to me through the Holy Spirit all that I need for a life that is filled to overflowing with joy, purpose, meaning, and satisfaction. I here and now accept Him as my personal Savior, Lord, and God. I lay aside all my pride and the things I have depended upon, and I look solely to You to be my complete Sufficiency.

And now . . . look for Christ Jesus to be your Sufficiency. I believe that if you have prayed this prayer with a sincere and humble heart, His presence, power, and supply will be revealed to you. Accept what He gives, and then freely pass it on to others!

☙ **Notes and Prayer Requests:** ☙

Notes and Prayer Requests:

Notes and Prayer Requests:

Notes and Prayer Requests:

Notes and Prayer Requests:

The Life Principles Series

STUDY GUIDES

Advancing Through Adversity
Becoming Emotionally Whole
Developing a Servant's Heart
Developing Inner Strength
Discovering Your Identity in Christ
Experiencing Forgiveness
Leaving a Godly Legacy
Listening to God
Overcoming the Enemy

Preparing for Christ's Return
Protecting Your Family
Relying on the Holy Spirit
Sharing the Gift of Encouragement
Talking with God
Understanding Eternal Security
Understanding Financial Stewardship
Winning on the Inside

Other Books by Charles Stanley

10 Principles for Studying Your Bible
Charles Stanley's Handbook For
Christian Living
Discover Your Destiny
Eternal Security
Finding Peace
The Gift of Forgiveness
How to Handle Adversity
How to Keep Your Kids on Your Team
How to Listen to God
In Step with God
Into His Presence
Landmines in the Path of the Believer

Living in the Power of the Holy Spirit
Our Unmet Needs
On Holy Ground
Pathways to His Presence
Seeking His Face
The Source of My Strength
Stuck In Reverse
Success God's Way
Walking Wisely
When the Enemy Strikes
When Your Children Hurt
Wining the War Within
The Wonderful Spirit-Filled Life